JOURNEYS

a journal for martial arts students

This publication is dedicated to the memory of

Mr. Mark Casey
1961 - 2014

on behalf of his students and their families.

GOALS
the achievements toward which efforts are directed

GOALS

Your present circumstances don't determine where you can go; they merely determine where you start.

Nido Qubein

GOALS

Goals allow you to control the direction of change in your favor.

Brian Tracy

GOALS

GOALS

You have brains in your head.

You have feet in your shoes.

You can steer yourself in any direction you choose.

You're on your own.

And you know what you know.

You are the guy who'll decide where to go.

Dr. Seuss

GOALS

GOALS

Set your goals high, and don't stop 'til you get there.

Bo Jackson

GOALS

GOALS

Goals seem impossible only when you are not heading toward them.

Mike Hawkins

GOALS

GOALS

The question isn't who is going to let me; it's who is going to stop me.

Ayn Rand

GOALS

GOALS

Difficult things take a long time, impossible things a little longer.

André A. Jackson

GOALS

GOALS

Obstacles are those frightful things you see when you take your eyes off your goal.

Henry Ford

GOALS

GOALS

The rung of a ladder was never meant to rest upon, but only to hold a man's foot long enough to enable him to put the other somewhat higher.

Thomas Henry Huxley

GOALS

GOALS

The journey of a thousand miles begins with one step.

Lao Tzu

ATTITUDE ~ SPIRIT
disposition and/or feelings about a person, thing, or
activity; orientation, especially of the mind

Today not possible, tomorrow possible.

Eternal Grand Master H.U. Lee

ATTITUDE ~ SPIRIT

Life shrinks or expands in proportion to one's courage.

Anaïs Nin

ATTITUDE ~ SPIRIT

Whether you think you can or think you can't, you are right.

Henry Ford

ATTITUDE ~ SPIRIT

A life is not important except in the impact it has on other lives.

Jackie Robinson

ATTITUDE ~ SPIRIT

Do not let circumstances control you. You change your circumstances.

Jackie Chan

ATTITUDE ~ SPIRIT

To give anything less than your best is to sacrifice the gift.

Steve Prefontaine

ATTITUDE ~ SPIRIT

Nothing can stop the man with the right mental attitude from achieving his goal; nothing on earth can help the man with the wrong mental attitude.

Thomas Jefferson

ATTITUDE ~ SPIRIT

I don't measure a man's success by how high he climbs but how high he bounces when he hits bottom.

George S. Patton

ATTITUDE ~ SPIRIT

I will love the light for it shows me the way, yet I will endure the darkness because it shows me the stars.

Og Mandino

ATTITUDE ~ SPIRIT

Weakness of attitude becomes weakness of character.

Albert Einstein

SELF-CONTROL

restraint of oneself or one's actions, words, etc.

SELF-CONTROL

Every action we take, everything we do, is either a
victory or defeat in the struggle to become what we
want to be.

Ninon de l'Enclos

SELF-CONTROL

Winners don't do different things, they do things differently.

Shiv Khera

SELF-CONTROL

Little said is soon amended. There is always time to add a word, never to withdraw one.

Baltasar Gracián

SELF-CONTROL

SELF-CONTROL

He who conquers himself is the mightiest warrior.

Confucius

SELF-CONTROL

The sense of dignity grows with the ability to say no to oneself.

Abraham Joshua Heschel

SELF-CONTROL

SELF-CONTROL

A little kingdom I possess, where thoughts and feelings dwell; And very hard the task I find of governing it well.

Louisa Alcott

SELF-CONTROL

SELF-CONTROL

The cyclone derives its powers from a calm center.
So does a person.

Norman Vincent Peale

SELF-CONTROL

SELF-CONTROL

Pain is weakness leaving your body.

Enson Inoue

SELF-CONTROL

Don't judge each day by the harvest you reap but by the seeds that you plant.

Robert Louis Stevenson

SELF-CONTROL

59

Nothing so conclusively proves a man's ability to lead others as what he does from day to day to lead himself.

Thomas J. Watson

PERSEVERANCE
steady persistence in a purpose, especially in the face
of difficulties, obstacles, or discouragement

PERSEVERANCE

I've missed more than 9000 shots in my career. I've lost almost 300 games. 26 times, I've been trusted to take the game winning shot... and missed. I've failed over and over and over again in my life. And that is why I succeed.

Michael Jordan

PERSEVERANCE

PERSEVERANCE

I do not think that there is any other quality so essential to success of any kind as the quality of perseverance.

John D. Rockefeller

PERSEVERANCE

PERSEVERANCE

Perseverance is not a long race; it is many short races one after the other.

Walter Elliot

PERSEVERANCE

PERSEVERANCE

There are no secrets to success. It is the result of preparation, hard work, and learning from failure.

Colin Powell

PERSEVERANCE

Don't be afraid to give your best to what seemingly are small jobs. Every time you conquer one it makes you that much stronger. If you do the little jobs well, the big ones will tend to take care of themselves.

Dale Carnegie

PERSEVERANCE

PERSEVERANCE

The drops of rain make a hole in the stone not by violence but by oft falling.

Lucretius

PERSEVERANCE

PERSEVERANCE

Luck is a dividend of sweat. The more you sweat, the luckier you get.

Ray Kroc

PERSEVERANCE

PERSEVERANCE

It isn't the mountains ahead to climb that wear you out; it's the pebble in your shoe.

Muhammad Ali

PERSEVERANCE

PERSEVERANCE

Pain is temporary. It may last a minute, or an hour, or a day, or a year, but eventually it will subside and something else will take its place. If I quit, however, it lasts forever.

Lance Armstrong

PERSEVERANCE

PERSEVERANCE

Opportunities multiply as they are seized.

Sun Tzu

LOYALTY
faithfulness to people and/or commitments

Be faithful in small things because it is in them that your strength lies.

Mother Teresa

LOYALTY

LOYALTY

Loyalty is something you give regardless of what you get back, and in giving loyalty, you're getting more loyalty; and out of loyalty flow other great qualities.

Charles "Tremendous" Jones

LOYALTY

LOYALTY

The function and duty of a quality human being is the sincere and honest development of one's potential.

Bruce Lee

LOYALTY

LOYALTY

Lack of loyalty is one of the major causes of failure in every walk of life.

Napoleon Hill

LOYALTY

LOYALTY

Loyalty means nothing unless it has at its heart the absolute principle of self-sacrifice.

Woodrow Wilson

LOYALTY

LOYALTY

Loyalty is still the same, whether it win or lose the game; true as a dial to the sun, although it be not shined upon.

Samuel Butler

LOYALTY

LOYALTY

The reputation of a thousand years may be determined by the conduct of one hour.

Japanese proverb

LOYALTY

LOYALTY

Loyalty is not what others expect of you, it is what you can give to others.

(unattributed)

LOYALTY

LOYALTY

Unless you can find some sort of loyalty, you cannot find unity and peace in your active living.

Josiah Royce

LOYALTY

LOYALTY

A faithful friend is a strong defense: and he that hath found such an one hath found a treasure.

Ecclesiasticus 6:14

RESPECT
esteem for the value of a person or thing

RESPECT

You can easily judge the character of a man by how he treats those who can do nothing for him.

James D. Miles

RESPECT

RESPECT

I fear not the man who has practiced 10,000 kicks once, but I fear the man who has practiced one kick 10,000 times.

Bruce Lee

RESPECT

RESPECT

Act as if what you do makes a difference. It does.

William James

RESPECT

RESPECT

Selfishness is not living as one wishes to live, it is asking others to live as one wishes to live.

Oscar Wilde

RESPECT

RESPECT

Every man must decide whether he will walk in the light of creative altruism or in the darkness of destructive selfishness.

Martin Luther King, Jr.

RESPECT

RESPECT

The Art of Peace is medicine for a sick world. There is evil and disorder in the world, because people have forgotten that all things emanate from one source. Return to that source and leave behind all self-centered thoughts, petty desires, and anger. Those who are possessed by nothing possess everything.

Morihei Ueshiba

RESPECT

RESPECT

To be one, to be united is a great thing. But to respect the right to be different is maybe even greater.

Bono

RESPECT

RESPECT

One should always treat others as they themselves wish to be treated.

Narayana, *Hitopadesa*

RESPECT

In the end we are all separate; our stories, no matter how similar, come to a fork and diverge. We are drawn to each other because of our similarities, but it is our differences we must learn to respect.

(unattributed)

RESPECT

RESPECT

Respect your efforts, respect yourself. Self-respect leads to self-discipline. When you have both firmly under your belt, that's real power.

Clint Eastwood

COURTESY
excellence of manners and/or social behavior

COURTESY

One of the sanest, surest, and most generous joys of life comes from being happy over the good fortune of others.

Robert A. Heinlein

COURTESY

COURTESY

Be kind whenever possible. It is always possible.

Dalai Lama

COURTESY

COURTESY

Whatever words we utter should be chosen with care for people will hear them and be influenced by them for good or ill.

Buddha

COURTESY

COURTESY

I can live for two months on a good compliment.

Mark Twain

COURTESY

COURTESY

I've learned that people will forget what you said, people will forget what you did, but people will never forget how you made them feel.

Maya Angelou

COURTESY

A wise man is superior to any insults which can be put upon him, and the best reply to unseemly behavior is patience and moderation.

Moliere

COURTESY

COURTESY

The only wealth which you will keep forever is the wealth you have given away.

Marcus Aurelius

COURTESY

COURTESY

Always keep an open mind and a compassionate heart.

Phil Jackson

COURTESY

COURTESY

Do not repeat anything you will not sign your name to.

(unattributed)

COURTESY

COURTESY

Really big people are, above everything else, courteous, considerate and generous - not just to some people in some circumstances - but to everyone all the time.

Thomas J. Watson, Sr.

HONOR
honesty and fairness in one's actions

HONOR

The only correct actions are those that demand no explanation and no apology.

Red Auerbach

HONOR

HONOR

We judge ourselves by what we feel capable of doing, while others judge us by what we have already done.

Henry Wadsworth Longfellow

HONOR

The coming of honor or disgrace must be a reflection of one's inner power.

Xun Zi

HONOR

HONOR

The shortest and surest way to live with honor in the world is to be in reality what we would appear to be; all human virtues increase and strengthen themselves by the practice and experience of them.

Socrates

HONOR

No person was ever honored for what he received.
Honor has been the reward for what he gave.

Calvin Coolidge

HONOR

HONOR

Quality is not an act; it is a habit.

Aristotle

HONOR

The least movement is of importance to all nature.
The entire ocean is affected by a pebble.

Blaise Pascal

HONOR

HONOR

He who has lost honor can lose nothing more.

Publilius Syrus

HONOR

Say not that honor is the child of boldness, nor believe thou that the hazard of life alone can pay the price of it; it is not to the action that it is due, but to the manner of performing it.

Pharaoh Akhenaten

HONOR

HONOR

It is not our purpose to become each other; it is to recognize each other, to learn to see the other and honor him for what he is.

Hermann Hesse

INTEGRITY
adherence to ethical principles; honesty

INTEGRITY

What lies behind us and what lies before us are tiny matters compared to what lies within us.

Ralph Waldo Emerson

INTEGRITY

INTEGRITY

Never separate the life you live from the words you speak.

Paul Wellstone

INTEGRITY

Real integrity is doing the right thing, knowing that nobody's going to know whether you did it or not.

Oprah Winfrey

INTEGRITY

INTEGRITY

The supreme quality for leadership is unquestionably integrity. Without it, no real success is possible

Dwight D. Eisenhower

INTEGRITY

INTEGRITY

You must be the change you wish to see in the world.

Mohandas Gandhi

INTEGRITY

Subtlety may deceive you; integrity never will.

Oliver Cromwell

INTEGRITY

Be a yardstick of quality. Some people aren't used to an environment where excellence is expected.

Steve Jobs

INTEGRITY

INTEGRITY

One of the truest tests of integrity is its blunt refusal to be compromised.

Chinua Achebe

INTEGRITY

Integrity is not a conditional word. It doesn't blow in the wind or change with the weather. It is your inner image of yourself, and if you look in there and see a man who won't cheat, then you know he never will.

John D. MacDonald

INTEGRITY

Integrity can be neither lost nor concealed nor faked nor quenched nor artificially come by nor outlived, nor, I believe, in the long run, denied.

Eudora Welty

LEADERSHIP

If your actions inspire others to dream more, learn more, do more and become more, you are a leader.

John Quincy Adams

LEADERSHIP

You do not lead by hitting people over the head. That's assault, not leadership.

Dwight D. Eisenhower

LEADERSHIP

LEADERSHIP

The final test of a leader is that he leaves behind him
in other men the conviction and the will to carry on.

Walter Lippman

LEADERSHIP

Things may come to those who wait, but only the things left by those who hustle.

Abraham Lincoln

LEADERSHIP

I start with the premise that the function of leadership is to produce more leaders, not more followers.

Ralph Nader

LEADERSHIP

As weather shapes mountains, problems shape leaders.

Warren G. Bennis

LEADERSHIP

A leader is a person you will follow to a place you wouldn't go by yourself.

Joel A. Barker

LEADERSHIP

all proceeds from the sale
of this publication will be donated to the

H.U. Lee
Memorial Foundation
huleefoundation.com

and the

Kick It Forward Foundation's
Mark Casey Memorial Fund
kickitforward.foundation

www.ingramcontent.com/pod-product-compliance
Lightning Source LLC
Chambersburg PA
CBHW062147280526
45788CB00001B/345